The Angler's And Sketcher's Guide To Sutherland

Archibald Young

THE

NGLER'S & SKETCHER'S

GUIDE

TO

SUTHERLAND.

BY

ARCHIBALD YOUNG, Advocate,

COMMISSIONER OF SCOTCH SALMON FISHERIES
AUTHOR OF "NOTES ON THE SCOTCH SALMON FISHERY ACTS OF 1862 AND
1868;" "SALMON FISHERIES," IN STANFORD'S SERIES
OF "BRITISH INDUSTRIES," ETC., ETC.

WILLIAM PATERSON, EDINBURGH.
67 PRINCES STREET.

1880.

PREFACE.

———o———

LAST summer a series of papers appeared in the *Scotsman*, entitled "An Angler's and Sketcher's Ramble through Sutherland." These have been carefully revised and considerably enlarged, and are now published in a separate form. They are the result of repeated visits to Sutherland, in the course of which it has been thoroughly explored; and it is hoped that they may prove useful to those who intend to visit a county which presents so many attractions to the tourist, the angler, and the artist.

EDINBURGH, *May* 1880.

CONTENTS.

---◆---

I.

CONTRAST BETWEEN THE COUNTY OF
SUTHERLAND IN THE 17TH AND 18TH
CENTURIES AND IN THE PRESENT DAY.
LAIRG; DORNOCH; GOLSPIE; DUNROBIN;
LOCH BRORA; THE BADEN LOCHS.

Contrast between the County of Suther-
land in the 17th and 18th Centuries
and in the present day.

MORE than two hundred years ago, Franck,
a Cromwellian trooper, whose "Northern Memoirs" were written in 1658, thus speaks of the
county of Sutherland :—"The next curiosity
to entertain you with is the county of Sutherland, which we enter by crossing a small arm
of the ocean from Tain to Dornoch. So
from thence we travel into Caithness, and
the country of Strathnaver, where a rude sort
of inhabitants dwell (almost as barbarous as
cannibals), who, when they kill a beast, boil
him in his hide, make a caldron of his skin,
browis of his bowels, drink of his blood, and
bread and meat of his carcase. Since few or
none amongst them hitherto have as yet
understood any better rules or method of
eating." In 1772, Pennant, the well-known
antiquarian and traveller, thus describes the
same county :—" I never saw a county that

seemed to have been so torn and convulsed;
the shock, whenever it happened, shook off
all that vegetates;" and in his "Tour through
the Highlands of Scotland," written some
fifteen years afterwards, Knox thus character-
ises it:—"The county of Sutherland is the
most remote in Great Britain, and also the
most rugged and least improvable. Excepting some considerable tracks along the shores,
it is mostly composed of mountains of rock
and strata, extensive morasses, and impas-
sable bogs. . . . The poverty of the soil
utterly precludes improvements in agriculture
of any consequence; and nine parts out of
ten in this great country must unavoidably
remain an inhospitable, sterile desert to the
end of time."

Franck, Pennant, and Knox, were they now
living, would be not a little surprised to see
the change that the lapse of time has wrought
in the county thus unfavourably characterised.
More than five hundred miles of good roads
now traverse it; a railway skirts its southern
and eastern borders; mail cars pass through
it from east to west and north to south;
comfortable and commodious steamers call
regularly at Lochinver, affording rapid and

ready communication with Glasgow and the
Clyde ; good inns are to be found within easy
distance of each other; a thriving tenantry of
sheep-farmers, owning 300,000 sheep, occupy
the straths and hills ; tourists flock to it every
summer, attracted by the wild beauty of its
lochs and mountains ; the agricultural improvements at Shiness, Baden Loch, Forsinard, and other parts of the county, com-
menced and carried out by the enterprise and
energy of the present Duke, have clearly
shown that many a seeming waste of barren
moorland may be converted into fertile pas-
ture, or made to bear good crops of corn and
turnips ; while the rental paid for its fishings
and shootings by sportsmen from all parts of
Great Britain is greater than the whole rental
of the county from every source at the time
when Knox and Pennant wrote.

Such a county is well fitted to charm the
tourist, the sportsman, and the artist ; and to
him who is both sportsman and artist it presents attractions such as can be found nowhere
else in Great Britain.   The angler, especially,
who is not rich enough to rent a salmon
river, will find it quite a fisherman's paradise.
The rivers, indeed, are let and preserved, but

the county is full of lochs, from Loch Shin,
more than twenty miles in length and a mile
wide, to the mere mountain tarn that covers
but an acre. Most of these abound in trout
of fine quality and good size; and, excepting
in the lochs in the deer forests, the fishing is
in general free. In the district of Assynt
alone there are said to be more than two
hundred and fifty lochs, and I have counted
seventy from the lofty summit of Quinag.

The artist will find himself not less well off
than the angler. On the southern border of
the county, the scenery is not remarkable for
beauty or grandeur. Yet along the course of
the Shin, in the neighbourhood of Dunrobin
and Golspie, and around Loch Brora, there
are good subjects for the pencil. The eastern
boundary is, on the whole, uninteresting; but
there are pretty spots in the Strath of Kil-
donan, and fine views of the twin summits of
the Ben Griams and of the graceful peak of
Morven in Caithness. The northern coast
between Melvich and Cape Wrath, facing the
stormy Pentland Firth, is bold and rugged in
outline, and affords splendid examples of rock
scenery; and there is capital sketching about

the Kyle of Tongue, above which rise the
grey ruins of Castle Varich and the serrated
ridge of Ben Laoghal, one of the most picturesque mountains in Sutherland. But it is
on the west coast that the artist will find the
best subjects for his pencil, especially in the
neighbourhood of Lochinver, Inchnadamph,
Aultnakealgach, and the Ferry House on
Loch Kylesku, one of the least known and
most beautiful of the many salt-water lochs
that indent the west coast of Sutherland, from
Cape Wrath to Inverkirkaig.

I entered Sutherland by Bonar Bridge,
beneath which the united streams of the
Shin, Oykell, Carron, and Cassley pour
their tribute of waters into the Dornoch
Firth. The channel of the river below Bonar
Bridge is severely and systematically netted
by net and coble during the fishing season.
The fishing belongs to Sir Charles Ross.
The Duke of Sutherland recently prosecuted
an action to limit the excessive exercise
of the right, but was unsuccessful ; and
there can be no doubt that the inevitable
result of the continued working of these
nets in the comparatively narrow channel

below Bonar Bridge, will be to inflict serious
and substantial injury on the angling in all
the four rivers above it. It is somewhat
strange, that though the Tweed Fisheries Act
of 1857, and the English Salmon Fisheries
Act of 1873, both contain provisions limiting
and restricting the working of net and coble,
there is no analogous provision to be found
either in the Scotch Salmon Fishery Act of
1862 or in that of 1868. Draught nets
may be worked night and day; and, while
one is coming in, another is going out,
so that the wonder is that any fish escape.
The remedy for this state of things, so
much and so justly complained of by the
upper proprietors in whose waters the fish
are bred, would be an enactment similar
to the 62nd clause of the Tweed Fisheries Act of 1857, or the 14th clause of
the English Salmon Fisheries Act of 1873.
The clause in the Tweed Act provides that
" Every person who shall shoot or work any
wear shot net in the river within the distance
of thirty yards of any other wear shot net
already shot or being worked in the river,
before such last-mentioned net is fully drawn

and landed, shall for every such offence be liable to a penalty not exceeding £5." The clause in the English Act—the last Salmon Fisheries Act passed by Parliament—is as follows :—"Any person who shall shoot or work any seine or draught net for salmon in a river across the whole width, or more than three-fourths of the width thereof, within one hundred yards from the nearest point in the line of shot of any other seine or draught net worked in like manner, and already shot or being worked in such river, before such last-mentioned net is fully drawn in and landed, shall for every such offence be liable to a penalty not exceeding £5." So far back as 1871, Messrs Buckland and myself, in our Report on the effect of recent legislation on the Salmon Fisheries in Scotland, recommended " that a clause should be introduced to modify the over-fishing by net and coble practised on some of the larger Scotch rivers."

The Shin, though it has a course of only six or seven miles from its great reservoir, Loch Shin to its mouth, is one of the largest and most important of the salmon rivers of Sutherland. It has a wide, full current, ex-

cept during very dry weather, and many
deep and spacious pools, some of which
have been judiciously formed or improved by
artificial means.   It is the earliest of the rivers
that enter the sea at Bonar Bridge, probably
owing to its higher temperature.   There is a
considerable fall some distance above its
mouth which seriously impedes, though it does
not entirely prevent, the ascent of salmon.
There is also a smaller fall about a mile
below.   Salmon seldom attempt to pass beyond the principal fall before the middle of
May, and there are at least a score of pools
between that fall and the mouth of the river
in which the spring angling is often first-rate.
After June, there is sometimes good fishing
in the upper section of the river between
the falls and Loch Shin.   The trout fishing
in the wide expanse of Loch Shin, both for
ordinary trout and *salmo ferox*, is fairly good.
There is an excellent inn at Lairg, close to
where the Shin issues from the loch.   At
Overskaig Inn, fifteen miles farther up the
loch, the trouting is better than at Lairg.
Salmon are rarely caught on Loch Shin; but,
on one occasion, when fishing near Overskaig,

I was fortunate enough to get two with the phantom minnow.

Owing to its being one of the chief stations on the Sutherland and Caithness Railway, and its piscatorial attractions, it seems not improbable that Lairg may ere long supersede Dornoch as the county town of Sutherland. Yet the ancient capital, though ten miles from Tain, the nearest railway station, and offering no temptations as a fishing centre, is well worth a visit. Its name is said to be derived from two Gaelic words meaning a horse's foot or hoof, the tradition being that, during a battle fought in the middle of the thirteenth century, William, Thane of Sutherland, after his sword had been broken, slew a Danish chief with a horse's leg which he caught up and used as a weapon. A horseshoe is still retained as the arms of the burgh; and at Earl's Cross, a little way from the town, a monument has been erected to commemorate the encounter. According to one historian, an army of Norwegians landed at the Little Ferry in Sutherland in 1240, and as they were marching to attack and plunder Dornoch, they were set upon by William Earl

of Sutherland, and Bishop Murray, at Hilltown near Embo, to the east of Dornoch.
After a desperate conflict the Norwegians
were cut to pieces, and their general was
slain.   He was buried at Hilltown, and a
stone was erected over his grave, which got
the name of " Croith an Righ," or the King's
Cross, as the common people fancied that a
king of Norway lay buried there.   A memorial
of this victory of the Sutherland men still
remains in the shape of a well-cut stone
which stands to the eastward of Dornoch.
On the north side are carved the arms of the
Sutherland family; on the south those of the
Bishop of Caithness; and on the top the
arms of the Bishopric.   With reference to this,
however, Mr Worsaae, in his account of the
Danes and Norwegians in Scotland, writes as
follows:—"Close outside the town of Dornoch,
on the east coast of Sutherland, there stands
a stone pillar in an open field, which is simply
the remains of one of those crosses so fre-
quently erected, in Roman Catholic times, in
market-places.   As a matter of course, the
arms of the Earls of Sutherland are carved on
one side of the stone, and on the other are

the arms of the town—a horse-shoe. Tradition, however, will have it that the pillar was erected in remembrance of a battle fought on this spot, in which the Earl of Sutherland commanded, against the Danes. In the heat of the battle, while the Earl was engaged in personal combat with the Danish chief, his sword broke; but in this desperate situation he was lucky enough to lay hold of a horse-shoe that accidentally lay near him, with which he succeeded in killing his adversary. The horse-shoe is said to have been adopted in the arms of the town in remembrance of this feat. In the Cathedral Church of Dornoch is a carved stone monument of the middle ages, representing one of the ancient Bishops who once resided in Dornoch. He also is said to have fallen in the same battle, but my authority, the person who shewed me over the Church, added,—'I am proud to say that the Danes were defeated!'"

The parish church of Dornoch is an interesting and handsome building. The original church, the date of whose foundation is unknown, was dedicated to Saint Finbar, a native of Caithness, and Bishop of Cork, who flourished, according to some authorities, in the sixth, and according to others, in the eleventh century. This building existed till the seventeenth century, when it was taken down or destroyed. It stood about the middle of the town of Dornoch, beside the cross, still existing. Close to it was the church built by Bishop Gilbert Murray in 1270, but which had fallen into ruins about the end of last century, and remained in that state until 1835, when it was rebuilt by the Duchess of Sutherland from the foundation, with the exception of the square central tower. As rebuilt, the church, within the walls, is of the following dimensions:—Length, 126 feet; height, 45 feet; length of transepts, 92 feet; side of square tower, 29 feet 6 inches. In the north transept is a stone sarcophagus removed from the choir, containing, it is said, the relics of Bishop Gilbert, whose figure is represented by a cross-legged effigy on the lid. Sixteen of the Earls of Sutherland are said to repose in the south transept. Besides this picturesque church, Dornoch can also boast of handsome County Buildings, consisting of court-house, prison, record-room, and

county meeting-room. These occupy the site
of the castle and palace of Dornoch, which lay
in ruins from 1713 to 1813. The high western
tower alone remains. Dornoch was erected
into a free royal burgh and port by Charles
the First in 1638, on the narrative that the city
of Dornoch was the only city of the earldom
and county of Sutherland to which, beyond
the memory of man, all the inhabitants of that
county flocked, as to a common emporium, to
purchase the necessaries of life; that, as a
place built near the sea-shore, it had a fit
station for a harbour for the importation and
exportation of merchandise; and that it was
expedient that it should be erected into a free
royal burgh and free port for the use of the
lieges in that part, which might be of much
use in reducing the barbarous and unculti-
vated mountaineers to civilisation. Dornoch
has long been famous for its beautiful links,
where the game of golf, now become so
popular, may be enjoyed in perfection. Sir
Robert Gordon thus writes of them in 1630:—
"About this toun, along the sea coast, their
are the fairest and largest linkes or green
feilds of any pairt of Scotland, fitt for

archery, goffing, ryding, and all other exercise ; they doe surpasse the feilds of Montrose or St Andrews." It will thus be seen that though Dornoch has been rather left out in the cold by the railway authorities, and although it is inferior as an angling station to many other places in the county, it has yet sufficient attractions of its own to render it well worthy of a visit.

The trout fishing in Loch Merkland, six miles from Overskaig, is far better than that on Loch Shin, and there is also good angling on Loch Griam, a smaller loch between Loch Shin and Loch Merkland. These three lochs are connected by streams in which there is occasionally fair fishing.

The trout in Loch Merkland are beautifully shaped and finely flavoured ; and as the loch is in general shallow, and has a gravelly bottom, they rise to the fly over a great extent of water, and on a favourable day take very freely. They average about three-quarters of a pound; but much larger ones are not unfrequently caught both with fly and minnow. There is no inn nearer than Overskaig.

On my way from Lairg to Golspie, I

examined the fish-pass on the Carnack, a tributary of the river Fleet, which falls into the Moray Firth near Golspie. It is one of the most remarkable salmon-ladders in Scotland, and enables salmon to ascend to Loch Buie, (which is two miles in length), in spite of a fall upwards of sixty feet in height. This fall has not been blasted, or in any way interfered with, the ladder enabling the fish to pass round the fall, and enter the stream at a point some distance above it. The ladder is about a mile and a-half above the junction of the Carnack and the Fleet; and Loch Buie, to which the fish run, is five miles farther up. The ladder was designed by the late Mr Bateson, of Cambusmore, and constructed under his direction; and he deserves much credit for this ingenious and successful device to overcome an apparently insurmountable obstruction. One noticeable feature in this ladder is that, after the salmon have taken several short jumps over steps not much exceeding a foot in height, they are provided with capacious resting pools in which to recruit their exhausted energies for the next series of jumps that await them. The retain-

ing walls forming the pools are roughly
but massively built of stones without mortar.
But the interstices are stopped with moss,
which arrests the silt carried down by the
stream, so that they soon become sufficiently
water-tight. In order to guard against the
risk of spates, a sluice is provided at the head
of the ladder, which prevents the admission of
more water than is required for the passage of
the fish. The total length of the ladder is
three hundred and seventy-eight yards, and it
is from ten to twelve feet wide. The salmon
are enabled to ascend an incline one hundred
and thirty-eight yards long, with a gradient
of about one in five, by means of a series of
pools, twenty-three in number. The remain-
ing part of the ladder is not so steep. There
are no pools in it, but only steps at intervals,
to break the force of the water.

A little to the east of Golspie, on a commanding site overlooking the wide waters of
the Moray Firth, stands Dunrobin Castle, the
magnificent residence of the Duke of Sutherland. The original castle is a building of
great antiquity. It has been absorbed and
modernised by the more recent alterations,

but still retains its characteristic features. Writing about two hundred and fifty years ago, Sir Robert Gordon thus describes it :— " It is a place situated upon a round mote, by which ther lyeth fair orchards and gardens, planted with all kynd of fruits, herbes, and floures used in this kingdome, and good store of safron, tobacco, and rosemarie. The fruit here is excellent, and cheaflie the pears. In the midst of the court within the castle their is one of the deipest draw-wells in Scotland, all made of aisler work from the ground, which was built and finished before the house was begun. This castle is situat hard by the sea." The earliest authentic notice of Dunrobin on record is about 1401, in which year Robert, Earl of Sutherland, granted a Charter at the Castle of Dunrobyn. Early in the sixteenth century, while Earl Adam was absent, Alexander Gordoun, the natural brother of the last earl who had in 1509 claimed the earldom, besieged and took Dunrobin; but, before a party sent by the Earl to raise the siege arrived, he had retired into Strathnaver, leaving a garrison in Dunrobin. They surrendered to Alexander Leslie of Kinninvy, who soon afterwards at

the head of a party attacked Alexander
Gordoun, and slew him near Kintradwell,
eight miles to the east of the castle. Leslie
beheaded Gordoun, and his head was carried
to Dunrobin, and placed upon the top of the
great tower. In 1567, Earl John and his
Countess, after being poisoned in the Castle of
Helmsdale, were carried to Dunrobin and died
there. In the same year Alexander, Master
of Sutherland, was seized, and kept for some
time at Dunrobin by George, Earl of Caithness, who is said to have dwelt there for a
time, and to have destroyed all the writs of the
family of Sutherland that he could find. In
1569, the Master was rescued by a stratagem
of his friends the Murrays and Gordouns,
who, in the absence of the Earl of Caithness,
concealed a party in Golspie glen, and contrived to inform the Master of their presence.
Thereupon he found means to elude the
vigilance of his captors and escape to his
friends. In 1580, Sir Robert Gordoun, the
historian and genealogist of the Sutherland
family, was born at Dunrobin. In 1650,
during Montrose's wars, the castle was strongly
garrisoned by the Earl, who retired into Ross-

shire ; and the governor of the castle having
captured some of Montrose's men, refused to
give them up ; but Montrose seems to have
made no attempt to capture the place. During
the present century extensive and splendid
additions have been made to Dunrobin ; but
the old castle, tower, and draw-well, though
incorporated in the new structure, have been
carefully repaired and preserved—the whole
constituting the princely seat of the present
Duke of Sutherland, the lineal descendant of
Hugh Freskin, who died about the year 1204,
and of whom Douglas thus writes in his
' Peerage of Scotland ' :—" He was one of the
greatest men in the kingdom, had vast pos-
sessions in lands in the counties of Moray,
Ross, Sutherland, and Caithness, which he
divided amongst his children, whose posterity
assumed their surnames from their posses-
sions, as was the custom of those early
times."

In the gardens attached to Dunrobin
Castle there is an admirably-constructed
museum, recently built, which contains a most
interesting collection of the birds, beasts,
fishes, antiquities, minerals, &c., which are to

be found in the county of Sutherland.   Here
may be seen some fine specimens of gold from
the Sutherland gold washings.   The beautiful
wooded glen of the Golspie burn, not far from
the castle, is well worthy of a visit.   A footpath leads up the glen for nearly a mile.   In
this glen ; on the banks of Loch Brora near
Craig Carrol; on the course of the burn which
runs into Loch Brora near Kilcalmkill; and in
the wild gorge between the Fall-pool above
Loch Brora and Castle Coll, the sketcher will
find many good subjects for his pencil.

Going by rail from Golspie northwards, I
passed the river Brora, an admirable angling
river, and a very early one.   In 1878, one rod
killed fifty-two salmon between the opening
of the season and the 1st of May.   The Brora
has long been famous for its salmon fishings.
In 1638, Franck thus writes of it in his
" Northern Memoirs " :—

" The next thing we meet with is the Lough Broroh,
that spouts forth a river into the bowels of the ocean.
This lough is deep, but not so large as the Ness (elevated in 59 degrees north latitude), but very full of
salmon ; and though the river seems to have rapid
streams, yet the tides influence them every twelve
hours.   I mention this Broroh for no other purpose

than to reflect on her plenty of salmon, where they barrel up for France and other parts annually (as reported) so much salmon as amounts to three hundred pounds sterling a-year; and the price of a salmon (among themselves) seldom exceeds one single denare."

Near Inverbrora, there is what might easily be made one of the finest golfing links in Scotland, as extensive as St Andrews, with beautiful velvet turf and plenty of hazards. On the seaward side of the links there is a beautiful sandy beach for bathing. The country round about is healthy and pleasant. A railway station is close at hand; and, in fact, a more favourable situation for a valuable addition to the number of our golfing links could scarcely be found.

Loch Brora is more than three miles in length, and consists of several stretches of water, of varying widths, united by deep, narrow, river-like channels. Its lower extremity is about four miles from the sea at Inverbrora. The river Brora flows into and issues from it. The loch contains salmon, sea trout, and yellow trout; but the salmon do not rise well to the fly. A good many years ago I resided on its banks for some weeks during several autumns, and fished it repeatedly. I never succeeded in getting a salmon; but on one occasion I got seventeen, and on another fourteen, sea trout in a day. The heaviest yellow trout I ever captured on it with the fly weighed three and a half pounds. Just about a year after I caught him, I got another only half a pound lighter from the very spot, outside a patch of reeds, where I had taken the first one.

A little way above Loch Brora, the river tumbles over a considerable fall, below which there is a deep and spacious pool, a capital lie for salmon. The spring salmon never attempt to pass above this fall; but in summer and autumn they ascend it, and I have taken three good fish in a day in autumn five miles higher up. Above the fall the river rushes through a rocky gorge, where there is a succession of, apparently, the most splendid pools. Yet no fish ever rises to the fly in them, though hundreds must pass through; and it is not until you emerge from the gorge, and get to where the stream again flows through a comparatively wide and level valley, that you have any chance of sport.

On the south shore of Loch Brora, near its lower extremity, there is an establishment belonging to the Duke of Sutherland for the artificial hatching of salmon. When I saw it, it contained about 340,000 salmon eggs from the Brora, Helmsdale, Thurso, and Rhine. There can be no doubt of the great advantages to be derived from the system of artificial hatching, though its benefits have not as yet been so thoroughly appreciated in this country as in Canada and in the United States. In Canada, the Colonial Government maintains seven "hatcheries," at an annual expense of £5000, which have turned out sixty millions of eggs and young fry of different kinds of fish into the lakes and rivers within the last ten years. There are similar establishments in the United States, and the Commissioner of Fisheries there has lately drawn up a volume of nearly a thousand pages on the subject of the propagation of food-fishes. By the artificial method we can do away, in a great measure, with the terrible risks to which the young fry bred in our rivers in the natural way are exposed ; as we can succeed in rearing smolts from at least three-fourths of the vitalised eggs placed in the breeding troughs, whereas, if these eggs had been exposed to the dangers of the river, more than three-fourths of the fry produced from them would never have reached the smolt stage. The breeding troughs used in the establishment on Loch Brora, at the time when I visited it, were the ordinary old wooden troughs, much more bulky and cumbersome than they need be. It would be a great improvement if troughs similar to those used by Sir J. R. S. Maitland in his great piscicultural establishment at Craigend, near Stirling, were substituted for them. These troughs are made of carbonised wood, perforated zinc, and glass rods. They take up little room, are light, neat, and convenient, and afford effectual protection against fungus, that great enemy of the pisciculturist.

About 10 miles north-east from the Brora is the fishing village of Helmsdale, where the river of that name joins the Moray Firth. This is a larger stream than the Brora, and the numerous lochs connected with its basin afford perhaps the best trout angling in Scotland. The spring salmon fishing in the Helmsdale is excellent. In 1878, up to 1st May, five rods killed two hundred and fifty fish. Among the lochs, Loch Leim-na-claven, Baden Loch, and Lochnaruar afford the best angling. In these three lochs the writer and two friends in five days killed with the fly six hundred trout, weighing over four hundred pounds. The best day's sport was got in Loch Leim-na-claven, at the foot of Ben Griam-More. The drawback to fishing in this loch is that it is situated six miles from Forsinard, the nearest inn, and that this distance must be traversed on foot, as no conveyance could be taken across the tract of wild moorland that leads to it. The trout in all the lochs in this district are red-fleshed and of very fine flavour. The tourist who stops at Forsinard should, if a fair walker, make a point of ascending Ben Griam-More, which commands one of the finest views in Sutherland; the eye, in a clear day, sweeping over the counties of Caithness and Sutherland, the Pentland Firth, and the Orkney Islands. A few miles from Forsinard Inn is the little loch of Sletill, situated in the midst of a dreary moor just on the borders of Caithness and Sutherland. The trout of this loch are remarkable for their size and quality, but are somewhat capricious. On a favourable day, however, twenty trout may be caught which will average a pound weight each; and a far greater number and weight have occa-

sionally been taken. Loch Sletill belongs to
the basin of the Halladale River, to which
also belong two other excellent lochs, Loch
Acron and Loch-na-Shealg. These lochs are
all late, July and August being the best
months.

Near the lower end of the Baden Loch there
is a capital subject for the sketcher. In the
foreground is a group of cottages, partly
thatched and inhabited, and partly in ruins,
with bare rafters and crumbling walls; beyond,
the Baden Loch and Loch-na-Clair form the
middle distance ; and the picturesque ridge
of Ben Laoghal and the still more distant
summit of Ben Hope make up a splendid
background. If the artist is a good walker,
and penetrates to Loch-na-Cuen, the most
remote of the Helmsdale lochs, he will find
some capital material for pictures at its northern
extremity, and also on the recently-made road
between Baden Loch and Syre, in Strathnaver.
There is no inn nearer than Forsinard, ten
miles off. But, if the sketcher can put up
with humble accommodation and plain fare,
David Mackay, the shepherd at Baden Loch,
can give him a comfortable room in his cottage,
and furnish him with a boat on the loch.

II.

FLIES, FISHING TACKLE, ETC.

Flies, Fishing Tackle, Etc.

THE flies I have found most deadly during
many visits to the lochs of Sutherland are the
following :—A bright red body with gold
tinsel, red hackle at shoulder, and teal wings ;
the same body with the brown feather of the
mallard for wings; claret or fiery brown body,
gold tinsel, red hackle at shoulder, and wings of
the mallard or bustard feather ; magenta body
with grouse wings and silver tinsel ; a green
body with gold tinsel, red hackle at shoulder,
small scarlet feather at tail—red worsted wont
do, as it looks black in the water—and teal
wings ; black body with silver tinsel, black
hackle at shoulder, and red tip at tail ; yellow
or orange body, with gold tinsel, red hackle at
shoulder, and teal or mallard wings. These
flies, along with the fly known as the " soldier
palmer," will form a sufficient variety of patterns for an angler's tour among the trouting
lochs of the county of Sutherland. The
barred and variegated feather of the Canadian

wood duck, and the half black, half white
feather, known to anglers as the hecham-
pecham, which forms part of the wing of the
mallard, will also be found to constitute killing lures if used in combination with any of
the above-mentioned bodies. The best size
for flies, according to our experience—though,
of course, the size should vary with the state
of the wind and sky, the fulness of the loch,
and other circumstances—is two sizes larger
than those commonly fished with on Loch
Leven in Kinross-shire. With regard to
trouting rods, I had two during my longest
visit to Sutherland, the one twelve the other
ten feet long, each made in two pieces, the
butts of white hickory, the points of washabaw,
a wood tougher than even greenheart. The
butts were rather slender, and the points
somewhat heavy. These rods were easily
used with one hand during a long day's fishing, and the smaller one was very convenient
for burn fishing, and for lochs where the trout
did not run large. Both rods cast a long line,
and, when playing a heavy trout, bent to
within eighteen inches of the grasp, thus
giving much greater power over the fish than

a rod with a butt as stiff as a lamp-post,
where the top joint or joints do all the work.
The only drawback to these rods is that the
length of the pieces makes them rather inconvenient to carry.   But besides these, I had a
walking-stick rod, thirteen feet long, which
I found very convenient for walking and
fishing among the more remote of the Sutherlandshire lochs.   The stiffness of the metal
butt was a disadvantage, and made it at first
somewhat disagreeable to fish with.   But this
feeling soon wore off, and it proved a most
useful servant.   I killed with it, during my
last tour in the county, upwards of six hundred trout from four pounds downwards.   Such
rods, however, to be of any use, require to be
most carefully made, and are, consequently,
rather expensive.   There is not much free
salmon fishing in Sutherland, most of the
rivers and a few of the lochs being let at high
rents.   But in Loch Assynt, Loch Awe, Loch
Shin, Loch Laoghal, Loch Garbet-beg, and
some other lochs, the tourist-angler has a
chance of getting a few salmon, grilse, or sea-
trout in the proper season, and also, in par-
ticular states of the tide, in the salt water in

the Kyle of Tongue and the Kyle of Durness.
For salmon fishing with fly from a boat, a
fifteen feet rod is quite long enough ; and,
indeed, a rod seventeen feet in length is
amply sufficient for any river in Sutherland,
except, perhaps, for parts of the Shin and the
Naver. As to salmon flies, the passing angler
will find the " Jock Scott," the " Popham,"
the " Childers," the " Durham Ranger," the
" Sweep," and the " Butcher," of different sizes
to suit the season and state of the water,
quite a sufficient variety of patterns. For
trolling from a boat, a stiff thirteen foot rod is
long enough. The natural bait is the most
deadly, especially for the *salmo ferox* or great
lake trout; and next to that the phantom
and protean minnows will be found the best.
For *ferox*, numbers nine and ten of the
phantom, either brown or blue, are not too
large. The protean is decidedly a better
imitation of a small fish than the phantom.
A flexible strip of lead passes through the
body of the minnow, and a gradual bend is
given to this, and so the spin is produced.
But this construction has the disadvantage
attaching to it—that if a fish seizes the min-

now and gets off without hooking himself,
you must haul in the thirty or forty yards of
line you have out in order to assure yourself
that he has not pulled the minnow straight,
and so destroyed its spin.

The Helmsdale river flows through and out of
a chain of large lochs, known as the Baden Loch,
Loch-na-Clair, and Loch-na-Cuen.   These
lochs cover an area of nearly two thousand five
hundred acres ; and the uppermost one, Loch-
na-Cuen, is very remote and inaccessible.   A
strange circumstance with regard to them is
this, that though the lowest of the series is little
more than twenty miles from the sea, and connected with it by the river Helmsdale, in
whose course there is no serious obstruction,
natural or artificial, to the passage of salmon,
it is yet a rare occurrence to catch a
salmon in any of them.   There is at least a
mile of splendid spawning ground on the
Rimisdale water, which flows into the north
end of Loch-na-Cuen, and it would be an experiment well worth making to establish
artificial breeding-troughs for salmon somewhere on that stream, in order to try if by that
means these lochs could be stocked with sal-

mon. The extensive breeding establishment of the Duke of Sutherland on the banks of Loch Brora, where there were three hundred and forty thousand ova from the Brora, the Helmsdale, the Thurso, and the Rhine at the time when I visited it, could easily spare the small stock necessary for such an experiment on the Rimisdale water.

The success of the attempt to reclaim the desolate stretch of brown moor at Shinness, which now bears good crops of oats and turnips, has induced the Duke of Sutherland to commence similar improvements in the neighbourhood of the Baden loch. The land there is, however, considerably higher above the sea than that at Shinness, and is liable to be swept by storms of wind and rain, so that, in unfavourable autumns, even if the crops came to maturity, they might not be got in. But the land, which has considerable capabilities, could probably be converted into good pasturage, so as to carry a much larger stock of sheep than at present.

Six salmon rivers, belonging to the Duke of Sutherland, fall into the North Sea between the Caithness March and Cape Wrath—the

Halladale, the Strathie, the Naver, the Borgie, the Hope, and the Grudie. Of these, the Naver is by far the best, and also the earliest. The angling on these rivers is let, and strictly preserved, and, except in very dry or exceptionally cold seasons, furnish good sport to the lessees. Most of them fall into deep bays, along the sides of which—chiefly along the western sides—the fish run in seeking the fresh water.

The fishing in the Halladale, the most easterly of these rivers, is best in spring; but is at all times uncertain, as the river soon floods and soon runs out, so that, in a dry spring or autumn, the angling is but little worth. The spring fishing is from the wooden bridge to the mouth of the river, a distance of about seven miles, in which space there are several good pools. After the month of June the salmon run further up, and the best fishing in summer and autumn is in the rocky pools between the wooden bridge and Forsinard. There is a tradition that Halladha, son of Ronald first Earl of Orkney, was slain in battle and buried in Strathhalladale, which has since borne his name. The scene of the battle is about the middle of the strath, near a place called Dal Halladha. Here the country people show a spot where a bloody combat took place between the Scots and Norwegians, on a hillside on the east bank of the river, now covered with cairns, where the dead were buried. A deep circular trench, twelve feet in diameter, with a large stone in the centre, on the other side of the river, marks the spot where Halladha and his sword were laid. Near the mouth of the Halladale there is a comfortable inn, with moderate charges, at Melvich. Close to Melvich is the fishing village of Port Skerra, where there used to be a considerable herring fishery, which has, however, fallen off, chiefly owing to the want of good harbour accommodation. There is deep water in the present harbour, but it is very limited in extent, and the entrance is narrow and dangerous from the proximity of rocks on either hand. It is a great misfortune that there are no harbours on this exposed and stormy coast between Thurso in Caithness and Loch Erribol in Sutherland, a distance of fifty miles. There are abundance of herrings of the finest quality off the north coast of Sutherland,

but there are scarcely any fishermen to capture
them.   An old fisherman at Port Skerra told
me that thirty years ago he had taken as
many as two hundred and thirty crans in
a season off that coast; and the late Captain Macdonald, commanding the " Vigilant "
schooner, belonging to the Board of White
Herring Fisheries, in the evidence he gave
before the Herring Fishery Commissioners
at Wick in September 1877, said :—

" Forty years ago there were excellent fishings between Cape Wrath and the Pentland Firth.
There are some parts of the coast from Cape Wrath
to Pentland Firth where the herrings are not fished.
The herrings are not fished there because the fishermen got into debt to the curers through want of
energy ; the curers declined to supply them with boats,
and the fishing was abandoned.   Whenever he passes
that part of the coast he verifies the fact that the
herrings are there by shooting gannets which are
feeding on them.   The failure there is due not to an
absence of fish, but to the fishermen not fishing."

In the Parish of Farr, in which Port Skerra
is situated, there are thirteen miles of sea
coast, composed either of bold rocks from
twenty to two hundred feet high, against which
the waves of the North Sea break with fear-
ful violence, or of shallow sands on which

heavy surges are generally rolling. Yet, on all this extent of coast, there is nothing worthy of the name of a harbour ; though at Kirtomy and Armidale, and in one or two creeks, boats may land in moderate weather. It is impossible to doubt that this want of harbour accommodation for fishing boats very much hinders the prosecution of the fishings of cod, ling, haddocks, and herrings, which abound off the coast, and that the establishment of a commodious and secure landing-place for boats would be a great boon to the district. Such an improvement might be made at no very great cost on the west side of Melvich Bay, where some rocks afford at this moment a partial and precarious shelter. The fishermen in the neighbourhood are all agreed that this would be the best position for a harbour.

The rock scenery around and to the westward of Port Skerra is singularly fine ; and, quite close to the inn at Melvich, the sketcher will find ample employment for his pencil. Deep coves, with lofty rocks, scooped into caverns and carved into pinnacles by the action of the North Sea waves, are to be found all along the rugged coast. Inland from Melvich Inn there

are several lochs which afford good trouting.
One of them—Loch Balligill—about three
miles distant, contains very fine red-fleshed
trout up to 3 lb. weight. There is no boat on
it, however, and it must be fished from the
sides, or by wading. Another loch—Loch
Meaddie—from which a good-sized burn runs
into Swordly Bay, also contains fine trout;
but it is fully ten miles distant from Melvich.

There is a pleasant road along the sea-
coast, from Melvich to Bettyhill, where there
is a good inn close to the mouth of the Naver.
The drive from Bettyhill to Aultnaharra, a
distance of twenty-seven miles, passes through
Strathnaver, along the banks of the river.
This is a rich, green valley, with here and
there a little birchwood. There are six beats
on 'the Naver, containing many fine angling
and resting pools, between the old cruive and
Loch Naver, let, at £100 per rod ; and, as it
is in contemplation to add a seventh beat
—from the old cruive to the chain boat—this
would bring the angling rental of the river
up to £700 a-year. And, in a favourable
year, the angling is well worth it, as many
as forty salmon having been taken on

this fine river by one rod in a fortnight. The
different beats are fished in rotation by the
anglers who have the river taken. The Naver
flows out of Loch Naver, a fine sheet of water
seven miles long, and in places more than a
mile wide. It receives two considerable
streams, the Mudale water and the Strath-
bagasty river, which afford good spawning
ground, and are ascended by salmon in the
autumn. Loch Naver lies at the foot of the
lofty Ben Klibrick, the second highest mountain in Sutherland. There is a good inn at
Aultnaharra at its upper extremity. The
loch contains salmon, grilse, and sea trout.
The chief angling season is from the opening of the fishing until May. March is in
general the best month. Fifty-two salmon
have been killed in seven weeks by a single
rod, and six in a single day. The chief
salmon fishing is at the upper end of the
loch, not far from the inn. The trout fishing on Loch Naver is indifferent. The best
trout fishing within easy reach of Aultnaharra
is in Lochs Meaddie and Laoghal. Each of
these is six miles distant; but there are good
driving roads, and conveyances may be had

at the inn.   The trout in both these lakes are
of very fine quality, and show capital sport.
Aultnaharra is the place from which the ascent
of Ben Klibrick is most easily made.   The
best way is to follow the road from the inn to
the shooting lodge near the head of the loch ;
from that keep along the moor at the back of
the sheep-farmer's house, and then strike off
to the right, up a gully or rift on the mountain side, which leads to the ridge, whence
the ascent to the summit is easy.   In clear
weather, the three seas that wash the shores
of Caithness and Sutherland can be seen from
the summit of Ben Klibrick.

I fished Loch Laoghal several times, and I
should be inclined to say that the best places
for trouting are the head of the loch, around
some islands on the eastern shore, and in the
bays near the shepherd's house opposite the
islands.   From the islands there is a capital
view of Ben Laoghal, with his craggy crown,
which I recommend to the notice of any
sketchers and anglers who may pause from
making war against the trout to take their
mid-day meal and smoke the pipe of peace
on these islands.   Loch Laoghal contains a

good many *salmo ferox*. A friend, who is
a most persevering and successful troller,
killed four in two days a couple of years ago.
weighing 8, 7, 5, and 4 lb. They were all
caught with large phantom minnows, numbers
8 and 9. Below Loch Laoghal is Loch
Craggie, a fine sheet of water; and below
that, again, is a much smaller loch—Loch
Slam—from which the river Borgie flows.
The trouting on both these lochs is good,
and salmon and grilse are not unfrequently
caught in Loch Slam, and occasionally in the
lochs above it. The largest loch trout (not
ferox) ever taken on Loch Craggie was killed,
fishing with worm from the side, by a smith,
of the name of Graham. This monster
weighed 8 lb., and the bay where he was
caught is still known as "Graham's Bay."

III.

ALTNAHARRA TO RICONICH.

Altnaharra to Riconich.

THERE is a good road from Altnaharra to Tongue on the northern sea coast of Sutherland. The distance is seventeen miles, and that part of the road which passes between the skirts of Ben Laoghal and Ben Hial, and Lochs Laoghal and Craggie, is highly picturesque. The Kyle and Valley of Tongue are almost surrounded by a semicircular sweep of mountains, of which Ben Hope, 3061 feet high, and Ben Laoghal, 2508, are the culminating points. Both are grand mountains; but the latter is decidedly the more graceful and varied in outline. From the Kyle; from the islands on Loch Laoghal; from the grass parks between the inn and the House of Tongue; from the valley of the Borgie,—it offers a splendid subject for the sketcher. Perhaps the best point of view is from the Kyle, where the grey ruins of Castle Varich, crowning a green promontory rising steeply from the water, form a fine middle distance for the picture. The inn at Tongue is remarkably well kept and comfortable.

There are two excellent positions in the
Kyle of Tongue for a fishing-boat harbour, so
much wanted on this exposed and stormy
coast. One, indeed, already exists at Scullamie, but it has proved a total failure from
the number of rocks that obstruct its entrance.
Between Scullamie, however, and the picturesque old House of Tongue, the residence of
Mr Crawford, the courteous and hospitable
factor for the district, there is an excellent
site, where a good harbour might easily be
constructed at a comparatively small cost by
utilising and adding to two reefs of rocks that
jut out into the Kyle, and already afford
partial shelter. On the opposite shore of the
Kyle, at Tolmine, there is a pretty and shel-
tered bay, which has a smooth beach and a fine
bottom, and affords easy access to the North
Sea. By erecting quays, and by connecting a
small island lying close by with the main-
land, this might be made a safe and commodious harbour. Herrings appear to have
been plentiful off this coast about one hundred
and forty years ago, as Knox tells us in his
"Tour through the Highlands of Scotland:"—

" I saw at Lord Rae's house in Loch Tongue a book

that contains copies of a correspondence, from the year 1730 to 1740, between George, Lord Rae, and certain merchants of Glasgow, Renfrew, and Dunbar, relative to herrings caught by his Lordship's tenants upon this coast. It appears from their correspondence that herrings were then plentiful; that his Lordship sold them ready cured; and that the merchants sent vessels to take them away at a fixed price agreed upon by contract between the parties, for a given number of years."

The ferry across the Kyle, which affords the only direct means of communication between Tongue, Loch Hope, Loch Erribol, the Kyle of Durness, and Cape Wrath, is exceedingly inconvenient, and gives rise to much delay. It is three-quarters of a mile wide. I crossed in a large open boat, which also took across my conveyance. The time occupied in crossing was nearly an hour, and in bad weather much longer time is required. The construction of about five miles of road, from the ferry pier along the west side, and round the head of the Kyle, to join the existing road near Kinloch Lodge, would be one of the greatest improvements that could be made to facilitate travelling in this part of Sutherland.

During my first visit to Tongue the weather was dry, and the angling consequently indiffer-

ent. One day I succeeded in capturing a
salmon on the Borgie, and I also got some
good trout on Loch Craggie and Loch Slam.
This year, however, I had better sport, getting
from 9 to 18 lbs. of trout per day, and one
day, on Loch Laoghal, capturing four trout,
whose united weight was 11½ lbs.

The greatest angling novelty at Tongue
this season has been the placing of a boat on
Loch Halm, a star-shaped loch, five miles in
circumference, lying to the south-west of Ben
Laoghal. It is thirteen miles distant from
Tongue Hotel, of which you can drive ten to
the shepherd's house at the head of Loch
Laoghal, and you must then walk the remain-
ing three over the hillside in a westerly direction. An indiarubber boat was tried on Loch
Halm for a day or two a few years ago, and
heavy baskets of beautiful trout were got;
but, with this exception, it has never been
fished from a boat, and as it is shallow, it
cannot be fished to advantage from the banks.
The day on which the boat was placed on
the loch was anything but a favourable one,
as the mist hung low on the hills, and the
wind was light and unsteady, while in the

afternoon continuous rain fell.   But, in spite
of this, the party from the hotel had capital
sport.   Only one of the six bays which form
the loch was fished with fly by two rods from
the boat; but the first hour and twenty
minutes, during which the wind was steady,
produced 17 lb. of beautiful trout.   Afterwards it became calmer, and heavy rain fell.
But the result of five hours' fishing was two
baskets containing 102 trout, and weighing
45 lb.   Much greater results may, however,
be confidently anticipated when Loch Halm
is better known and fished in more favourable
weather.   It cannot be fished from the hotel
after the beginning of August without the
permission of the shooting tenant on whose
ground it lies.

There is a very pleasant excursion to be
made from Tongue to Dun Dornadilla, in
Strathmore, but it takes a long summer's day
to do it, as the distance there and back is
nearly forty miles, and the double crossing at
Tongue Ferry entails a great loss of time.   A
large burn falls into the west side of the Kyle
near the ferry.   There are some deep pools on
it in which sea trout of considerable size are

occasionally captured. The road from the
ferry to Loch Hope runs for eight miles along
a bleak moor, and about half-way stands a
solitary house, called the Moin House, or
house on the moss ; but the scenery changes
for the better near the shooting lodge on the
river Hope. This is beautifully situated, and
commands magnificent views up and down
the valley. Like most of the shooting lodges
in Sutherland, it is built of wood, covered with
slates. The river Hope rises in the deer
forest of Stack, and after a course of several
miles, falls into Loch Hope, a picturesque
sheet of water, six miles long, containing salmon, grilse, sea trout, and common trout. A
short, broad stream connects Loch Hope with
Loch Erribol, a spacious arm of the sea, affording the best anchorage in the North of Scotland. The drive along the side of Loch Hope
is very pretty, especially at the entrance to
Strathmore. On one side are bare hills, and,
on the other, every ledge and knoll is covered
with beautiful natural birchwood, above which
rise the steep rugged sides of Ben Hope.
There are some fine salmon pools in the
Strathmore river in the three miles of its

course between Castle Dornadilla and Loch
Hope. Near the keeper's house, a considerable
burn termed the Alt-na-Caillach, runs into the
Strathmore river from a lofty plateau on the
shoulder of Ben Hope, nearly one thousand
feet above the road. From this plateau the
burn plunges over a perpendicular face of rock
at least three hundred feet in one leap. From
the road only the upper portion of the fall is
visible; but, on ascending to the plateau, you
see its full magnificence. There is no check
or break in the headlong sweep of the falling
water. Sheer down it goes in one leap into
the deep pool below. From the top of the
fall a good walker will reach the summit of
Ben Hope in an hour and a-half. The local
tradition is, that an old woman had followed
her calf, which had strayed to the moor at the
top of the fall. There she caught it; but the
calf bolted with the old woman clinging to it,
and plunged over the fall, when, strange to say,
the old woman escaped, while the runaway
calf was killed. Hence the name of the burn,
Alt-na-Caillach, or burn of the old woman.

Not far from this burn is a fine specimen
of the circular Duns which appear to have

been very numerous in this part of the Highlands, the ruins of no fewer than ten existing
in the single parish of Durness. This one in
Strathmore is the most perfect. It is called
Dun Dornadilla—that is, Dornadilla's tower
—the tradition being that it was built by a
Scottish king of that name, and used as a hunt-
ing residence. It is about sixteen feet in height
and fifty yards in circumference, and consists
of two concentric walls built of slaty stones.

The Hope is a later river than any of those
that run into the Pentland Firth to the eastward of it. Indeed, it may be said that with
the Hope the late rivers begin; as all the
rivers westward from it to Cape Wrath, and
southward from Cape Wrath along the west
coast of Scotland up to the head of the Scotch
shore of the Solway Firth, are, with scarcely
an exception, late; whereas, almost all the
rivers eastward of the Hope, between it and
Duncansby Head and southward between
Duncansby Head, and the Tweed, are early.
The cause of this lateness or earliness I be-
lieve to arise from the relative temperatures
of the fresh water of the rivers, and of the sea
into which they fall. I stated this theory in

letters to the *Scotsman* in October and November 1875, and afterwards more fully in my Treatise on " Salmon Fisheries " in Stanford's series of " British Industries." The Scottish rivers flowing into the German Ocean are almost all early rivers. They have comparatively long courses, and fall into the sea at considerable distances from their mountain sources, after running for some part of their career through districts not greatly elevated, and possessing a moderate climate. But the German Ocean, into which these rivers flow, is a cold sea; and in winter and early spring the river temperature is, in ordinary seasons, much the same as that of the sea, and, therefore, salmon ascend these rivers early in the season. Take the Tay, for example. It is well known that salmon run into it in great numbers in the months of December and January, so that, when the fishing begins in February, Loch Tay is stocked with clean and heavy salmon. On the west coast, on the other hand, the rivers that fall into the Atlantic are all late. They have short courses, and their sources are much tilted up, as they rise in that lofty and singularly picturesque chain of mountains which, beginning not far from Cape Wrath, skirts the shores of Sutherlandshire, Ross-shire, and Invernessshire, for more than a hundred miles, at distances varying from five to twenty miles from the western sea.   In winter and spring these mountains are snow-clad, and every partial melting of their snows brings down torrents of ice-cold water, which rush through the short channels of these rivers into the sea. But the water of that sea, unlike that of the German Ocean that washes our eastern shores, is warmed by the soft influence of the Gulf Stream, and the salmon consequently prefer to remain in it until the snow-water has run off, and the milder weather of June and July has raised the temperature of the river waters, and then they begin to ascend.

With regard to the rivers flowing into the Pentland Firth, the Hope and Grudie are comparatively late, while the Borgie, Naver, Strathy, Halladale, and Thurso are decidedly early rivers.   But that distinguished naturalist, Sir Wyville Thomson, is inclined to think that an arctic current passes down the west side of the Orkneys, striking against the

north coast of Scotland at a point somewhere
about Loch Erribol, into which the Hope
flows, and that this cold sea extends all along
the north coast to the eastward of the Hope;
whereas, to the westward of this point, the
influence of the Gulf Stream makes itself felt.
In the former case, the rivers, owing to the
causes above explained, are early; in the
latter they are late. I understand that Sir
Wyville Thomson intends ascertaining by
careful soundings the position and extent of
this arctic current, which he supposes to flow
southwards through the trough between the
Faroe Islands and Shetland and Orkney, and
to be cut off from the warmer sea to the west
by a ridge which extends from the neighbourhood of Cape Wrath to the southern shoals
of Faroe. He states that at a station to
the east of this line the bottom temperature
at 450 fathoms is 31° Fahrenheit, and at a
station to the west about 40°.

In order to test the correctness of the
theory above stated, careful and prolonged
observations on the relative temperatures of
several late and early rivers, and of the sea
into which they fall, will be necessary, by

means of maximum and minimum thermometers. Such observations are now in the
course of being made by the Scottish Meteoro-
logical Society, at their station at Inverugie
on the east coast, and by the Duke of Sutherland on two early and two late salmon rivers
within his county. A very ingenious and
beautiful apparatus has recently been invented
by Mr Thomas Stevenson, C.E., for observations of sea and river temperatures by means of
thermometers continuously immersed. If the
result of such observations, carried on for a
sufficient length of time, shall be to prove the
correctness of the theory above stated, we
shall at last obtain something approaching to
a scientific method of determining the annual
close time suitable for each river. Another
result will be to prove the futility of all
attempts to change late rivers into early ones
by stocking them with salmon bred from ova
taken from early rivers. For, if the theory
with regard to the constant and invariable
effects of the relative temperatures of the sea
and of the rivers which fall into it, upon the
earliness or lateness of the ascent of salmon
be correct, it seems quite clear that all such

attempts are a mere waste of time and money.
As long as the physical characteristics of the
river proposed to be converted from a late
into an early salmon river, and of the sea at
its mouth remain unchanged, the mere intro-
duction of fish taken from an early river will
have no effect, and will result not in trans-
forming late rivers into early ones, but in
changing the fish taken from the early river
into late fish. The river will modify the
habits of the fish, but the fish will never
change the character of the river.

From Tongue to Durness is a long journey
of thirty miles ; and as there is no inn on the
road, the tourist is obliged to take corn along
with him, and to rest and feed his horse at
some convenient spot by the roadside. The
river Hope is crossed by a chain ferry boat.
A steep hill leads up from this ; and, two
miles farther on, Loch Erribol is reached.
At the time of King Haco's expedition to
conquer Scotland in the middle of the
thirteenth century, Loch Erribol was called
Goas fiord, from an island near its entrance
termed Goan or Hoan. During a plundering
expedition sent on shore in the vicinity of

E

Loch Erribol from the Norwegian ships, the
invaders were surprised by the natives,
headed by an officer of the king of Scotland
who resided in Dornadilla's tower. Most of
the strangers were slain, and among them the
commander of the party, called Urradall, who
has given his name to Strath Urradale. The
best anchorages in this splendid and spacious
sea-loch are in a bay, where there are the ruins
of an old church, and above an island, green
as an emerald with an encircling narrow strip of
yellow sand separating the verdure from the
water. Extensive quarries of limestone are
wrought not far from Church Bay, and several
vessels were shipping lime at the time when
I passed. Between twenty and thirty years
ago Loch Erribol used to be famous for its
lobsters, as many as ten thousand having been
taken from it in a single season. This fishery
has, however, greatly fallen off, and the loch
would appear to be almost fished out. Many
years ago a party of yachtsmen are said to
have played rather a malicious trick on the
lobster fishers of Loch Erribol. They drew
up a number of the lobster creels, took out
the lobsters, boiled them, replaced them in

the creels, and put them back into the loch.
When the fishermen came to take up the
creels, to their astonishment and horror they
found them full of boiled lobsters; and the
consequence was, that they believed the loch
to be bewitched, and it was some time before
they would venture to resume their fishing.
The mountains at the head of Loch Erribol are
singularly bleak and bare; but the valley of
the little river Polla, which runs into the head
of the loch, is very fine, with steep crags frown-
ing over it, and a considerable growth of
birchwood on the banks of the stream.   I
stopped to rest the horses near the bridge
over the Polla. Between the bridge and the
junction of the river and loch there are some
good pools. Out of one of them, black, deep,
and with a fine stream flowing through it, I
managed to take a four pound sea-trout and
several smaller ones during the time the
horses were resting and feeding. The Whitten
Head, on the east side of Loch Erribol, is
remarkable for its towering height and white
colour, and for the multitude of caves, some
of them extending a long distance, which the
waves have hollowed out in its base. It forms

a conspicuous landmark for the storm-tossed
mariner, and points out the entrance to a quiet
haven. By far the most interesting object
between Erribol and Durness is the Smoo
Cave, which well deserves a visit. The cave
may be reached, either by a pathway leading
from the high road, or by the sea, from which
the approach is by a narrow creek between
precipitous walls of rock. The entrance is
under a lofty arch, like the portal of some
vast Gothic cathedral, and, within, the cave
expands to a height and breadth of nearly a
hundred feet. At some distance inwards
from the entrance a small stream falls
through a rift in the rocky roof of the cavern,
and forms a still, deep pool in its bosom,
more than seventy feet below. This pool is
thirty yards across, very deep, and is separated
from a smaller and outer pool by a low ledge
of rock, over which those who desire to penetrate to the recesses of the cave must get a
boat lifted and placed in the inner pool. After
crossing this they will find themselves close
to a narrow low-browed archway, not above
three feet in height, under which they must
pass lying flat in the boat. From this they

enter a lofty vault covered with stalactites overhanging another dark still pool nearly as extensive as that which they have just left; and, if inclined to penetrate still deeper, they may walk on to the termination of the cavern, about a hundred feet beyond the farther extremity of this innermost lake. There is a spot a few yards distant from the high road where you may stand upon the roof of the cavern, a deep chasm on either hand, through one of which the stream which supplies the silent sunless pools below leaps into the cave.

The river Grudie or Dionard falls into the sea near Durness. It rises at the foot of Mealhorn, and some of the most stupendous precipices in Sutherland overshadow its source. It is a late river, there being but little fishing before June, and the chief run of grilse being in July. The angling is sometimes very good when the river is in order. The keeper at Gualin House told me that he had seen fourteen salmon taken and nine lost by a single rod in one day. The best patterns of flies are the "Popham" and "Captain," the latter being a yellow-bodied fly with yellow wings,

something like the "Childers," but brighter.
The innkeeper at Durness rents the four
miles of the Grudie nearest the sea. There
are some beautiful pools at and below the
bridge over the river about four miles from
Durness. The rock scenery of the coast in
the vicinity of Durness is magnificent, especially about Cape Wrath, Far-out-Head, and
Whitten Head—the rocks rising from two
hundred to seven hundred feet in perpendicular height. There are two lochs not far
from the inn—Lochs Borlay and Craspul—
both of which contain excellent trout. The
former also abounds in char, which, however,
will not rise to the fly. Char, indeed, are to
be found in scores of the lakes in Sutherland,
but as a rule do not take the fly. I once
killed three on Loch Borrolan while fly-fishing for trout, but this is rare. But there is
one small loch of the purest spring water high
up on the shoulder of Ben Hope, where this
shy and beautiful fish is said to take the fly
freely, and a small grey fly is reported to be
the most attractive lure. The fishing for sea-
trout in the Kyle of Durness, spinning with
the sand eel, is occasionally first rate. This

season one gentleman had four capital days—
his worst day being thirteen sea-trout weighing 20 lbs., and his best forty, weighing 68 lbs.

From the bridge over the Grudie, a long
steep hill leads up to the summit of the road
between Durness and Riconich Inn. Here
stands a solitary and exposed building, called
Gualin House, where the keeper resides, and
where the lessee of the Grudie finds accommodation when he comes north for the angling
season. The house was originally built as a
shelter for travellers who might happen to be
benighted in this dreary spot in stormy
weather. For some distance above the bridge,
the Grudie pursues a winding course till the
eye loses sight of it in the rocky recesses of the
wild Strath Dionard. Salmon and sea trout
ascend to Loch Dionard, in which it has its
source. I was told by the keeper at Gualin
House that the grandest rock in Sutherland is
a little beyond Loch Dionard. He estimates
its height at one thousand feet perpendicular.
It is distant about eight miles from Gualin
House, and the way to it is very rough. The
views of Ben Spionn (2566 feet) and of Foinaven (3015 feet) are very striking as you ascend

the hill to Gualin House. On the descent
from Gualin House to Riconich, also, many picturesque views open out, especially one, where
long lines of dark rocks, ridge beyond ridge,
stretch away towards the western sea.   A
little below Gualin House, on the left of the
road, is Loch Taravie, where good trout fishing is occasionally got.   The keeper at Gualin
has a boat upon it.   Nearer Riconich, on the
right of the road, there is a large burn,
called the Achriesgill water, with at least a
mile of capital spawning ground, from which,
however, salmon and sea trout are excluded
by a fall near its mouth.   But the fall is to be
blasted, with the view of opening up this valuable stretch of spawning ground.   This burn
runs into Loch Inchard, the northernmost of
the many beautiful sea-lochs which so deeply
indent the west coast of Sutherland.   Riconich
Inn is pleasantly situated at the head of Loch
Inchard, about half-a-mile from where the
river of the same name flows into it from
Loch Garbet-beg. The distance between this
little fresh-water loch and Loch Inchard is
only about a mile and a-half, and a pleasant
and well-made path leads up from the high

road by the banks of the Inchard to the boat-
house at the foot of Loch Garbet-beg. There
are no obstructions on the Inchard worth
speaking of, and salmon and sea trout find
their way easily into Loch Garbet-beg. The
fishing season is late—from June onwards.
Tourists staying at Riconich Inn have the
privilege of fishing in Loch Garbet-beg and
the adjoining lochs and streams. As many as
forty salmon have been killed in the loch by a
visitor at the inn during a single season. The
stream which connects Loch Garbet-beg and
Loch Garbet-more is a mere burn, with some
deep holes with good spawning ground in
them. The construction of a dam and sluices
at the head, so as to let down an artificial
spate if necessary, in order to induce fish to
ascend in dry weather, would probably enable
salmon to pass into Loch Garbet-more more
freely than they can do at present, during the
fishing season. Loch Garbet-beg is a shallow
reedy loch ; Loch Garbet-more is comparatively deep and clear. It contains large
yellow trout, and the *salmo ferox* has occasionally been caught in it. There is a very good
point for a sketch of Loch Garbet-beg and

the grey towering mass of Arkle, one of the
mountains of the Stack Deer Forest, on the
path up the side of the Inchard, a little below
the boat-house.

IV.

RICONICH TO LOCHINVER.

Riconich to Lochinver.

RICONICH INN is a good residence both for the sketcher and the angler, and the mountain air is wonderfully pure and exhilarating. I stayed a few days there in the end of May, a month too early for the fishing, especially as the season had been a very dry one, and both the Inchard and Loch Garbet-beg were at their lowest level. Yet, as the weather was bright and fine, I spent my time very pleasantly, driving about the neighbourhood, and wandering on foot in the huge, wild corrie that runs along the steep grey slope of Foinaven, and extends to the foot of Arkle. In this corrie, which is about three miles long by one wide, there is a perfect nest of lochs, all containing trout, and there are splendid views to be had of the grand mountains of the Stack Deer Forest. About four miles from the inn there is a good subject for a picture, where a small loch, with some rough moorland, broken up by grey rocks, occupies the foreground, and

the distance is formed by Arkle and Stack—
the former rounded and massive in outline,
and the latter towering up in a sharp and
graceful peak.   Both Foinaven and Arkle
may be conveniently ascended from Riconich.
On the latter, much caution is requisite in
walking, as there are steep beds of loose
stones in many places, which are easily set in
motion, and are apt to bear down with them
the unwary pedestrian.   An excellent trouting
burn runs out of the lowest of the Foinaven
lochs into Loch Garbet-beg.   It is called the
Garavalt, and has a course of nearly a mile.
About half-way up there is a considerable
waterfall, and below and above this there are
a number of capital pools and streams, in
which very nice trout up to a pound in weight
are to be found.   Twice during my stay, by
using fine tackle and small flies, I managed
to extract twelve pounds' weight from it, although the water was low and clear.   There
is a good cast just where the burn joins Loch
Garbet-beg.

At Kinlochbervie, about four miles from
Riconich, there is a fresh-water loch connected
with the sea by a short burn.   Near the mouth

of this burn there is a fall which prevented the
ascent of salmon and sea trout into the loch.
This has, however, been recently blasted, and
when the burn is high the fish are able to get
up. But it would be an improvement to widen
the entrance to the cut that has been made,
and to form a subsidiary dam below the pool
into which the water from the cut falls. This
dam should be about three feet high, and there
are plenty of boulders lying close at hand with
which it could be made. Such a dam would
have the effect of raising the water on the face
of the fall, so that fish would have no difficulty
in ascending. I got a boat and fished the
loch from which this burn runs, catching,
among other fish, a sea trout of a pound and
a-half, the first, I was informed, that had been
caught since the blasting of the fall. This
loch seems very deep, especially on the side
next the high road, and would suit well for
trolling. From the highest point of the road,
before reaching Kinlochbervie, there is a
splendid view of the fine sweep of mountains,
consisting of Foinaven, Arkle, and Stack.

Another day, during my stay at Riconich,
I went to fish a loch about a mile and a-half

from the inn, not far from the high road leading to Scourie. It is connected with an arm
of Loch Inchard by a short burn, and an
attempt has been made to clear and deepen
its course, so as to allow salmon and sea trout
a free entrance to the fresh water. I was
informed that this attempt has been successful, and that sea trout three pounds in weight
have been taken in the loch; but, unfor-
tunately, I had no opportunity of testing this
for myself, as the day was so bright and calm
that it was useless to cast a fly.

A pleasant excursion may be made from
Riconich to Sandwood Loch, a large expanse
of water, with its lower extremity close to the
western sea. The small river Shinary flows
into the head of the loch. There was once a
salmon-fishing station on the sea-shore near
this loch, and salmon used to enter it from
the sea; but the fury of the westerly gales
has silted up its communication with the
salt water to such an extent that no fish
can now ascend, so that the fine spawning
ground in Strathshinary is at present utterly
unproductive.

You can only drive as far as the schoolhouse beyond Kinlochbervie, and you must then walk about four miles across a very boggy stretch of moorland in order to reach the Shinary and Loch Sandwood, passing several small lochs by the way. I struck the river about a mile from where it enters the loch. There are some good rocky pools in this part of the stream, and some deeper ones three miles farther up. There is also a considerable extent of spawning ground. Near its junction with the loch, the Shinary becomes deep and still. Loch Sandwood is a large sheet of water, covering at least a square mile. The south side is very deep all along, until quite close to the sea, where it gets shallower, and there are large boulders in many places close to the beach—just the sort of shore where salmon and sea trout would like to lie. The north side is also deep, and the loch is in general free from weeds; so that it would be a splendid loch for trolling were salmon enabled to ascend. It contains very large trout. They have been caught five pounds' weight with the fly; and in the river Shinary, trout of two and three pounds are often taken by the people in the neighbourhood. There was

F

a mere rill of water running from this fine
loch through the sand into the sea when I
saw it, up which not even a small sea trout
could have found its way. It is a great pity
that a better communication could not be
made between Loch Sandwood and the sea.
The south side, close to the foot of a ledge of
steep rock, would be the best place to make a
channel.

A pleasant road, passing round the head
of Loch Laxford—a name derived from two
Norwegian words (*lax fiord*), meaning salmon's
firth—and crossing the famous river of that
name, not far from its junction with the salt
water, leads from Riconich to the village of
Scourie where there is a comfortable inn.
"Laxford" is only one out of many examples
that might be cited of the names of places in
Sutherland derived from the Norwegian.

In the north of England, and in the low-
lands of Scotland, the Scandinavian colonists
were chiefly Danes. But in the Scottish
Highlands, in the Orkneys and Shetlands,
and in the western islands, they were almost
entirely Norwegians. This was natural, as
these localities were much nearer Norway than

Denmark, and the sea-lochs and hills of Scotland, though on a smaller scale, might well
remind a Norwegian of the fiords and mountains of his native land ; and so it happened
that the Norwegians founded settlements on
the north-west coasts of Scotland and in the
Hebrides that subsisted for centuries after
the extinction of the Danish power in England. Orkney and Shetland were conquered
by them in the ninth century, and colonized in
the ninth and tenth ; and from these islands
expeditions in search of plunder were made to ·
the adjacent parts of Scotland, and particularly
to Caithness and Sutherland, which finally re-
sulted in their conquest. King Harold Har-
fager gave the Orkneys as an earldom to be
held under the crown of Norway to Ragn-
wald More Jarl's family. This family produced several distinguished men, who extended
their dominion over large territories in Scotland. Jarl Sigurd the Stout, who was married
to a daughter of the Scottish king, Malcolm
Canmore, and Jarl Thorfin his son by that
princess, were especially conspicuous. They
carried their conquests as far south as
Moray. Thorfin was the last of the

Orkney Jarls in whom the old viking spirit
lived and stirred. His power was greater
than that of any of his predecessors or
followers. According to the Sagas, he ruled
over eleven earldoms in Scotland, over
all the Hebrides, and over a considerable
kingdom in Ireland. He died about 1064.
Sigurd was the first conqueror of Sutherland,
and extended his conquests as far as the river
Oykell, which still forms the boundary of
the county. He is said to have met his
death in rather a curious way. He had defeated and slain a Scottish earl in battle,
and had cut off his head and fastened it to
his saddle, but a projecting tooth in the head
chafed his leg as he rode along in triumph,
and inflicted a wound that ultimately proved
fatal. It seems quite natural, therefore, that
Norwegian names should still be everywhere
found in Sutherland, such as those ending in
dale, the Norwegian equivalent for strath or
valley, like Halladale, Helmsdale, Swordale,
Armidale; and those terminating in boll, that
is, dwelling or farm, such as Kirkiboll, Torboll,
&c. Four of the great sea-lochs in Sutherland are still called by Norwegian names—

the Kyle of Tongue, from the Norsk tunga,
a tongue of land ; Loch Erriboll and the large
farm of Erriboll, that is the boll or dwelling
on the eir or point of land, from the old Norsk
eyri ; the Kyle of Durness from naes or ness
a promontory ; and lastly Loch Laxford,
that is the salmon firth, from lax a salmon and
fiord a firth. The name of the picturesque
mountain in the parish of Eddrachillis and of
the loch from whose shores it rises abruptly
for more than two thousand feet, are likewise Norwegian, " stack " meaning a precipitous rock rising from the sea. In Caithness,
too, Norwegian names are even more common
than in Sutherland. Thus, in the numerous
words which end in *ster*, we find the Norse
soetr, — that is, farm or sheiling. Thus,
Ulbster is Ulv's or Olaf's-soetr; Thrumster is
Thors-soetr; and soon with Scrabster, Lybster,
Stemster, &c. Then there is the Norse *gio*,
meaning a small bay or firth, which we find
in many places in Caithness, as, for example,
in Fresgio or Freyas-gio, in Girnigo, Ruigo,
Staxigo, and other localities that might easily
be mentioned. The Scandinavian *vik*, meaning bay or haven, is also easily recognised in

many parts of the county; for instance in
the town of Wick and in Freswick, and Dar-
wick; and in *Forss* we find the Norse for
waterfall, while in Thurso we have Thor'saa
or the river or water of Thor. The famous
Norse sea-rovers were termed vikings on
account of their frequenting the viks or
havens to watch for passing ships.

Below Laxford Bridge there is a deep and
rocky pool up to the foot of which the tide
flows. The length of the Laxford between
Loch Stack and Loch Laxford is only three
miles; but in that short distance there are
about a dozen capital pools. The Laxford
is a late river, the fishing season not commencing until the month of June. Both the
Laxford and Loch Stack go with the Stack
Deer Forest, and are strictly preserved. The
sea-trout on Loch Laxford are numerous, and
of a large size—five pounds and upward being
not an uncommon weight.

There is not much good trout fishing in
the immediate neighbourhood of Scourie.
But at Badcaul Bay, about five miles distant,
there is a small stream connected with a
chain of fresh-water lochs, in which the trout

are numerous and excellent. The high road
to the south crosses this stream, but there is
no driving road to the lochs, to which the
angler must walk. There are no fewer than
eleven lochs connected with this stream.
The two nearest are about a couple of miles
from Badcaul Bay ; and the most remote lies
at the foot of Ben Auskaird.

One of the most beautiful drives in Sutherland is that from Scourie to Overskaig Inn,
on the banks of Loch Shin. It is a long
day's journey—between thirty and forty miles
—and the best place to stop to rest is at
the hamlet of Achpharle, at the foot of
Loch More. There is no inn on the road,
as the greater part of it passes through the
deer forest of Stack, a wild tract of seventy
thousand acres of towering mountains, deep
corries, and sequestered lochs, the haunts of
the red deer and the ptarmigan. There are
some points on this road, as you approach
Ben Stack from Scourie, where that mountain
has exactly the appearance of the Matterhorn
in miniature. A very striking part of the road
is that portion of it which runs for a couple of
miles between the foot of Ben Stack and Loch

Stack. On the right are the rocky buttresses
of the mountain, and on the left the waters of
the loch, with just the breadth of the road between them.   From Achpharle, where the
horses rest, by far the most conspicuous ob-
jects in the landscape are the grand precipices
on the south side of Arkle, which form a rocky
wall some miles in length, and from one hundred to six hundred feet in height.   A small
river unites Loch More with Loch Stack.
The former is a fine expanse of water, with a
beautiful beach of white gravel.   It contains
large and excellent trout, but is strictly preserved.   On its banks stands Loch More
Lodge, the commodious and picturesque
summer residence of the Duke of West-
minster, the lessee of the Stack Forest.
Beyond Loch More, you pass the water shed
and come down upon Loch Merkland, which
is open to the public, and contains plenty of
beautiful red-fleshed trout, which sometimes
attain two or three pounds weight.   This,
again, is united by a pretty stream with Loch
Griam, a smaller loch, which discharges its
surplus waters, by a short channel, into the
great reservoir of Loch Shin.

After leaving Scourie, I travelled to the
very comfortable inn kept by Mr Maclachlan
at Lochinver. This is a long but beautiful
and varied drive of between thirty and forty
miles.   By far the grandest scenery on the
road is around the ferry-house on Loch Kylesku, and on the steep ascent that leads up
from it along the side of Quinag.   The people
at the Ferry House are civil and obliging, and
they have fitted up a comfortable parlour,
and can accommodate a couple of anglers or
artists who are content with plain fare and
lodging.   For an artist in search of Highland
scenery of the wildest and grandest description, there could be no better situation than
the ferry-house at Loch Kylesku.   This loch
penetrates very deeply into the land, and
above the ferry-house it divides into two
branches—Loch Glendhu and Loch Glencoul
—the former three miles, and the latter five
miles long.   The head of the latter is scarcely
ten miles distant from the head of Loch Shin,
whose waters discharge themselves into the
Dornoch Firth.   All around these lochs there
is a ring of grand mountain, beginning on
the north with Ben Strome, and sweeping

round to Quinag on the south, the circle being
filled up by Ben Leod, the stack of Glencoul,
Ben Uie, and Glasven.   There are two small
rivers with lochs connected with them, which
fall into Loch Glendhu.   Late in the season,
and after a fall of rain, not only common
trout, but also sea-trout and grilse may be
got in them.   The only way to reach them,
however, is by boat from the ferry-house on
Kylesku.   There is said to be a waterfall,
six hundred feet high, on a stream that runs
into the head of Glencoul.   I stopped for
some time on the roadside between the ferry-
house and the top of the hill leading up towards Loch Assynt, to make a sketch of the
grand corrie and peaks of Quinag, the highest
of the mountains that look down upon Loch
Kylesku.   There is a view of Quinag almost
equally fine on the other side from the road
between the foot of Loch Assynt and Lochinver.   From that side it seems nearly
inaccessible, as a long range of precipices,
culminating in sharp peaks, extends unbroken
for several miles.   The views of Loch Assynt,
while descending from the summit of the road
to the Loch, are very beautiful.   Its southern

shore is clothed with natural birchwood,
and beyond, the sharp summits of Canisp
and Suilvean form a telling background.
Near the foot of the loch is the handsome
shooting lodge of Mr Whitbread, not far
from the dark crags of Quinag, and yet em-
bosomed in thriving birch woods. After
leaving Lochinver, the road for some miles
skirts the wooded banks of the Inver, a late
river, but one which in wet seasons sometimes
affords good salmon angling. The innkeeper
at Lochinver rents part of it, and lets it out
to tourists staying at the hotel at the rate of
twelve and sixpence a day for each rod.

V.

LOCHINVER, INCHNADAMPH, AND ALTNAKEALGACH.

Lochinver, Inchnadamph, and Altnakealgach.

LOCHINVER is the chief place in the parish of Assynt, a parish extending over nearly a hundred thousand acres, very mountainous and rugged, and containing at least two hundred lochs, large and small. Some idea may be formed of the number of lochs when it is stated that within a circle of four miles' radius, measured from the village of Lochinver, upwards of fifty lochs are to be found, almost all abounding in trout, and free to the public. The outline of Assynt is very irregular; indeed, its name is said to be derived from the Gaelic compound *as agus innte*, signifying out and in. The mountain scenery cannot be surpassed in the British Isles. From Loch Kylesku, on the north, to Altnakealgach Inn, on the borders of Ross-shire, on the south, we find range after range of picturesque mountains— Quinag, Suilvean, Canisp, Glasven, Benmore, Brebag—wonderfully varied in form and

character. The culminating point is Benmore, the highest mountain in Sutherland,
whose summit rises three thousand three
hundred feet above the sea.

Rather more than four miles from the inn,
the route being chiefly along the road to Loch
Assynt and a short walk over the moor, lies
Loch Beanoch—a loch literally teeming with
trout, which rise freely to the fly. They are
not very large—running about three to the
pound—but, in the course of a day's fishing, a
few of a pound weight, or even heavier, may
be expected. The quality of the trout is
excellent; and, on a good day, a basket of
six or seven dozen may easily be taken. On
one occasion I took five and a-half dozen
in less than four hours. At the southern
corner of Lochinver, a small river, called the
Culag, joins the salt water close to the splendid
lodge which the Duke has recently erected
near the pier where the steamers from Glasgow call every fortnight. This river has but
a short course, and issues from a small fresh-
water lake. There are, however, several good
pools on it; and both in them, when the river
is in order, and in the loch, sea trout and

grilse may occasionally be got after the month
of June. Above this loch and connected with
it by a small stream is a second, with a wooded
island in it. From this loch is, perhaps, the
best point in the neighbourhood of Lochinver
from which to sketch Suilvean. This singular
mountain, which rises steeply above Loch
Fewin from a table-land of rugged gneiss hills,
has been termed the "sugar-loaf" by mariners,
from its regular conical shape when seen from
Lochinver and from other points on the coast.
It may be ascended both on the north and
south sides by a sort of rift or gully between
two peaks; but from all other points it is
inacessible. It is advisable to take a guide.

A pleasant drive from Lochinver is that to
the bridge over the river Kirkaig, close to
which is a gate opening on the footpath that
leads to the falls, two miles up the river, which
at present effectually bar the ascent of salmon
to the fine pools and spawning ground on the
Upper Kirkaig, and to the long chain of lakes
which extends across the parish of Assynt
into the county of Ross. The falls are at
least fifty feet perpendicular; and as the
banks, both above and below for a consider-

G

able distance, are steep and rugged, it would
be an enterprise entailing great difficulty and
expense to open up the long stretch of lochs
and river above by tunnelling or blasting.
The river Kirkaig here forms the boundary
between Ross-shire and Sutherland. There
are a number of fine pools and streams on the
Kirkaig, between the falls and Inverkirkaig;
but as the spawning ground is so limited by
the falls, it can never become an angling river
of much importance until that obstacle shall
be overcome. Above the falls, and between
them and Loch Fewin, is about a mile of
river, with some splendid deep, rocky pools,
such as salmon love. Beyond this, again, is
Loch Fewin, a long, narrow loch, whose waters
lave the range of low rugged hills above which
rise the steep sides of Suilvean. It is a capital
trouting loch, and large *salmo ferox* have been
caught in it by means of set lines, baited with
a good-sized trout. I twice fished it with
fly. On the first occasion I killed sixty-six
trout, weighing twenty-five pounds, chiefly
with a green-bodied fly with gold tinsel and
teal wings. On the second occasion, there
was a cold east wind, and I was not nearly

so successful. This year two rods captured two hundred and forty trout in one day, averaging about four to the pound. The best points for sketching Suilvean from Loch Fewin are just above the place where the boat belonging to Lochinver Hotel is kept, and about half-way up the loch from the side opposite the mountain. In the former case, you have the loch in the foreground; a group of low hills covered with scanty vegetation, and thickly dotted over with reddish gray boulders beyond; and in the distance the chief peak of Suilvean and the two lower summits behind. In the latter, the loch is again in the foreground; the rounded group of gneiss hills on the other side forms the middle distance; while the ridge of Suilvean, stretching from north-west to south-east, fills up the view. From the point where we made this sketch, the path, or rather rift in the mountain-side, that leads to the top of Suilvean, is quite visible; and after crossing the lake, a good pedestrian would have no great difficulty in making the ascent. Some of the boatmen furnished by the landlord of the Lochinver Hotel are quite capable of acting as guides. From the foot of Loch Fewin there is a short cut across the hills to Lochinver, by which the hotel may be reached in an hour and a-half's walking. A beautiful river, about a mile long, runs from the foot of Loch Veattie into the head of Loch Fewin. In its course are three fine pools and as many streams, that would be favourite haunts of salmon, if they could only be passed over the Falls of the Kirkaig. The trouting at present is first-rate, the fish being both numerous and large, and it is open to the public.

About seven miles to the south of the pretty village of Lochinver, lies a wide sheet of water encircled by a girdle of grand mountains and studded with numerous islands, one or two clothed with a rich covering of grass and ferns, and adorned by the white stems and graceful foliage of the birch, but by far the greater number rocky and barren. This highland loch and its surroundings present as wild and magnificent scenery as is to be found in Scotland; and those who are fortunate enough to obtain leave to fish in it will find the trouting of a first-rate description, the fish being both numerous and large. The name of the

loch is by no means a pretty one, being printed
" Skin-a-Skink ; " but in the speech of the
natives it is somewhat improved, being pro-
nounced as .if it were spelt " Shin-a-Shiag."
It does not belong to the county of Sutherland ; but it may, nevertheless, be appro-
priately included in the present sketch, as it
is the largest loch in the extensive estates
belonging to the Duchess of Sutherland in the
county of Cromarty. Its general shape is
square; but its shores are in many places
indented by deep bays, and its entire circumference cannot be much under fifteen
miles. Around this wide expanse of water
rise the steep precipices of Suilvean ; the
rocky sides and sharp summit of Coulmore ; and the rounded shoulder with its
crest of serrated rock that is known as
Stack Polly. The large island in the centre
of the loch is a prominent object in the landscape with its groves of natural birchwood
and its green carpet of grass and ferns. The
deer from the forest around the lake occasionally swim across to rest and feed in this
sylvan paradise. The long wall or dike that
forms the crowning ridge of Stack Polly

extends for nearly a mile along the south
shore of the loch. It is toothed and jagged in
the most fantastic and extraordinary way.
On the side next the loch it forms a sheer
precipice, varying in height from thirty to
three hundred feet. The summit is accessible,
but the ascent is both difficult and dangerous,
especially the last part, where you have to
walk for some yards along a narrow ledge of
crumbling rock with a lofty precipice on
either hand. A false step here would be certain destruction.

I have twice fished Loch Skin-a-Skink, and
though on both occasions the weather was
unfavourable, there being too much rain and
too little wind, I was successful in getting
some very large trout. When fishing it along
with a friend about three years ago, our two
largest trout weighed respectively twelve and
six pounds. The twelve-pounder was a
splendid specimen of a *ferox*, and was caught
in rather a remarkable way. My friend had
been trolling with a No. 8 phantom minnow,
and was hauling it in in order to get a three-
quarters pound trout that had taken it. When
his tackle was about ten yards from the boat,

there was a sudden rush through the water, and then a tremendous pull on the line caused by the twelve-pound *ferox* who had made a dash at the trout already hooked on the phantom minnow, but in so doing had contrived to hook himself. He fought well and made several desperate rushes before he gave in; but after about twenty minutes struggle we got him into the boat. As it turned out, we caught no fewer than three trout at one haul, namely, the trout originally hooked on the phantom, the twelve-pound *ferox*, and a half-pound trout which we found inside the ferox when we cut him up. But by far the finest basket of trout I ever saw taken out of Loch Skin-a-Skink was caught by a friend who had a day's leave in the summer of 1878. There were only eighteen trout, and they were all caught by trolling. But the eighteen weighed thirty-six pounds. The largest was six pounds; but they were all splendid fish, and when spread out on the stone slabs in front of Lochinver Hotel, they formed quite a picture to charm an angler's eye.

The lower end of Loch Skin-a-Skink is about three miles from the sea, with which it is connected by the small river Polly which falls into Enard Bay at Inverpolly. The Polly has a winding course of about two miles from the lowest loch from which it issues to the sea, and it flows through three lochs after its exit from its great reservoir, Loch Skin-a-Skink. All of these are probably good trouting lochs, and the uppermost one is between two and three miles in circumference. There were no boats on any of these lochs at the time when I visited them, and their trouting capabilities remain yet to be ascertained.

A small river flows into the head of Loch-Skin-a-Skink, having previously passed through four lochs in its course. I fished this stream one day with the fly and got some beautiful trout both in size and quality from it and from Loch Kynoch, from which it issues. On the north shore of Loch Skin-a-Skink, and connected with it by a large burn, lies Loch Achyle, the head of which is within less than half-a-mile of the river Kirkaig above the falls. Altogether there are no fewer than eleven lochs, including Loch Skin-a-Skink, belonging to the catchment basin of the river Polly, and almost all these might be opened up for salmon and sea-trout by making the falls on the Polly passable. At present, they form a complete barrier to the ascent of fish. An outlay of £500 would probably effect this, and such an outlay would be most amply repaid by the increased rental of the fishings were the series of streams and lochs once opened up for salmon, instead of being frequented by trout only. There is some capital spawning ground on the Polly, both above and below the falls. The lower falls are about a mile and a half from the sea. They are two in number, about twenty yards apart. I examined them during a very dry season, when there was but little water in the river; and at that time the height of the lower fall was about eight, and of the upper about fourteen feet. By far the easiest and cheapest method of getting salmon up would be to bring them round these falls, for which there are great natural facilities : as, immediately above the upper fall, the river splits into two branches, the larger passing over the falls, and the smaller running through a narrow channel, with a comparatively easy gradient, and join-

ing the main stream below the lower fall.
This channel should be enlarged and deepened,
and the main body of the stream diverted
into it, which would soon widen the passage
for itself, so that salmon and sea-trout would
be able to ascend. These falls are immediately
below the loch nearest to the sea, from which
the Polly issues. The next fall is on the
stream between the first and second loch, and
is a far more formidable obstacle, being quite
twenty feet high, with a break or step in the
centre, the banks for some distance below
being perpendicular rock. At present, this fall
forms a complete and insurmountable obstacle
to the ascent of salmon and sea-trout. It would,
however, be practicable to lower the upper
half of the fall by blasting with dynamite, and
to form a channel or ladder in the rock on the
left bank of the stream up to the middle of
the fall where a resting pool should be constructed. Of course, if these falls should ever
be made passable, and Loch Skin-a-Skink and
the other lochs belonging to the basin of the
Polly opened up for salmon, it would be
advisable, nay, almost necessary, to combine
with these improvements an establishment on

a moderate scale for the artificial breeding of salmon on some of the upper waters—for example, on the stream running into the head of Loch Skin-a-Skink from Loch Kynoch.

Loch Crokach, about three miles from Lochinver Hotel, contains trout handsome in shape, and of fine quality. There is likewise a loch near Storr Bay where they are got of large size and delicate flavour ; and in Loch Clashmore, about seven miles from the hotel, they are sometimes caught three pounds in weight. But to enumerate the trouting lochs in the vicinity of Lochinver would be an endless and tedious task ; for the whole country between the northern sea-board of Assynt and Lochinver, a distance of about eight miles in a straight line, is literally honeycombed with lochs, on many of which a fly has probably never been cast. This naturally arises from the wildness and inaccessibility of the country. There are no roads in the interior, and the only high road passes round the coast.*

* Since the above was written, the accommodation for tourists at Lochinver has been very much extended and improved. The old inn, near the northern angle of the bay remains as it was ; but, in addition to this,

A pleasant drive of seventeen miles, running
along the banks of the Inver and between the
shores of Loch Assynt and the steep sides of
Quinag, brings the tourist to the comfortable
inn of Inchnadamph, lying at the foot of one
of the buttresses of Benmore, the loftiest
mountain in Sutherland. Here the angler or
sketcher would do well to rest for a week.
The scenery is magnificent, and the fishing
excellent and varied. Close to the inn there
are numerous fine subjects for the pencil, and
for those farther off good conveyances will
be supplied by the innkeeper at a reasonable
rate ; for the days are gone by in which an
old tourist wrote of Sutherland :—" It is a
country where no man who cannot climb like
a goat and jump like a grasshopper should
attempt to travel." Inchnadamph inn stands
on a gentle slope between the small rivers

the Duke's beautiful lodge at its southern corner is
now converted into an hotel under the name of the
" Culag Hotel," so called from the small river that falls
into the sea close to it. There is now accommodation
for sixty tourists. Both inns are in the hands of Mr
W. Burns Brown, who has salmon and trout fishing to
let, and also shooting extending over twelve thousand
acres.

Loanan and Traligill, both of which flow into
the head of Loch Assynt—the former from
Loch Awe and the latter from the sides of
Benmore. These two streams, as well as Loch
Assynt, Loch Awe, and Loch Mulack-Corrie,
are open to the public. The angling season is
late, not commencing until the month of June.
The Traligill, which is little more than a good-
sized burn, nevertheless contains numerous
and beautiful trout. I have taken six dozen
in a day with fly, from a pound weight downwards, when the water was in good order.
After a short course through a steep and picturesque glen, it disappears in the mountain.
Beyond the point where it disappears, the
hillside rises abruptly, and proceeding up
this for some distance, you come to a chasm
where you hear the sound of subterranean
waters, which, on stooping down, you can see,
at a great depth below, rushing along in white
foam, over steep rocks. Still further up the
hillside you meet a second chasm, where the
imprisoned waters are also visible and audible,
chafing along at the bottom of the cavern.
After an hour and a-half's steep walking from
the inn, you reach a sort of tableland from

which the precipices of Benmore rise grandly towards the north, while a range of steep grey limestone rocks bounds it towards the east. Here there is a small loch, shallow and weedy, but which contains the finest trout, in fatness and flavour, that I have ever met with. They feed on the fresh-water shrimp which abounds in the loch. I have never taken them above three pounds in weight, but I have heard of their being caught of a much larger size. The general run is considerably smaller. They are shy and capricious, and somewhat tender in the mouth, so that they require to be treated delicately on being hooked. They take both fly and worm. There is a boat on the loch ; but it may be easily fished from the side by wading. It is called Loch Mulack-Corrie, and it is also known as the " Gillaroo Loch." The trout in it have an indurated stomach ; but both Mr Stoddart, the well-known writer on angling, and Mr Stirling, of the Anatomical Museum of Edinburgh University, are of opinion that they are not the true gillaroo trout. During the two days on which I fished this loch, I got five trout weighing six pounds, and nine trout weighing seven pounds. They were all caught with fly, and I found a bright red body, with gold tinsel and teal wings, the most deadly. Mr Sutherland, the innkeeper at Inchnadamph, a fisherman of great experience, and thoroughly acquainted with the district, maintains that these trout spawn in the loch about Christmas time, and that they have never been seen either in the burn that flows into, or in that which runs out of it.

Every sketcher who goes to Inchnadamph should ascend to Loch Mulack-Corrie for the sake of the unrivalled view of Benmore which is to be had from the head of the loch. I twice made a sketch of it in water-colours from that point, and was strongly impressed with the perfect picture which nature placed before me. On the way back to the inn, there is a capital subject of quite a different character, on a large burn that flows into the right bank of the Traligill through a rocky gorge, with some natural wood and a thatched cottage near its head.

Besides common trout and the great lake trout, the ample expanse of Loch Assynt

contains in the season grilse and sea trout.
For grilse and sea trout, the best locality is
the rocky shore below the high road between
the head of the loch and Ardvreck Castle;
for the great lake trout, the steep wooded
crags on the opposite shore, beneath which
the water is very deep; and for common
trout the bays around and below Ardvreck
Castle. On the south shore of Loch Assynt,
not far from the head, there is a point where
the loch; Inchnadamph Inn; the hill behind
it; and the towering summit of Benmore combine to form an attractive picture. But by
far the finest view of Loch Assynt to be had
in the neighbourhood is from a point between
the inn and Ardvreck Castle, where a bay of
the loch; the picturesque old castle on its
rocky peninsula; the bold peaks and grey
rugged sides of Quinag; and the wide expanse of the loch beyond, bounded by lower
hills; afford admirable materials for a picture. Ardvreck Castle was erected about the
end of the sixteenth century by the Macleods,
who were then Lords of Assynt, and appears
to have been once strongly built and well for-
tified. It was a Neil Macleod, owner of this

stronghold, who, pretending friendship, got the Marquis of Montrose betrayed into his Castle, after his defeat at Corbiesdale, near Invercarron, in 1650, and then delivered him up to his enemies. Not far from Ardvreck Castle, and also on the shores of Loch Assynt, stands the ruins of Calda House, a more modern residence, built by the Mackenzies who succeeded the Macleods as lairds of Assynt. It was destroyed by fire about a hundred and thirty years ago, and nothing but the bare walls now remain.

Loch Awe, a small loch about a mile long, lying at the foot of Canisp, four miles from Inchnadamph, is by far the best trouting loch in the vicinity of the inn. It is close to the high road from Inchnadamph to Altnakealgach, so that the angler can either drive or walk to it ; or if he prefers it, he may fish up the Loanan, which connects Loch Awe and Loch Assynt, and which, in the latter part of the season, contains grilse and sea-trout. The best pools are at and above a wooden bridge over the Loanan rather more than half-way to Loch Awe. On the left of the road leading to Loch Awe there is a stupendous ridge

H

of limestone rock extending for a mile and a half. The precipices are more than 200 feet in height, and are, in places, mantled with ivy. Loch Awe contains several wooded islands, and is a shallow weedy loch, where trolling is almost impossible; but the trout take the fly so freely that this is not of much consequence. We found the " soldier palmer" a very deadly fly on this loch. The following is a return of seven days' fishing on Loch Awe at different times in June and July, several of the days being by no means favourable ones: — fifty-one trout, three weighing a pound each ; thirty-six trout ; thirty-one trout ; sixty-six trout, weighing twenty pounds; fifty-five trout, weighing eighteen pounds ; sixty-three, weighing nineteen pounds ; eighty-seven, weighing twenty-seven pounds. This gives an average of fifty-five trout per day, which considering the beauty and quality of the Loch Awe trout, is not bad sport.

After leaving Inchnadamph, we drove to Altnakealgach Inn, situated on the shores of Loch Borrolan on the very borders of the counties of Sutherland and Ross. The distance between the two places is eight miles.

Like Inchnadamph, Altnakealgach is capital
headquarters both for the angler and the
sketcher. Lochs Borrolan, Cama, Urigill, and
Veattie, the Ledmore and Ledbeg rivers,
the stream issuing from Loch Urigill, and
some other streams, can all be conveniently
fished from this inn, and are all open to
tourists. How productive these lochs occasionally are, may be judged from an entry in
the visitors' book at Altnakealgach, dated
some years back, in which the writer states
that, in ten days' fishing, during the month of
August, he caught one hundred and five dozen
trout with the fly. Then, as to sketching,
there is a beautiful view of Suilvean from the
road or the shores of Loch Borrolan, a little
to the east of the inn. From various points
on the banks of Loch Urigill, Coulmore,
Coulbeg, and Suilvean are seen to great
advantage. The black falls between Cama
Loch and Loch Veattie afford an admirable
subject. From one of the wooded islands
on Cama Loch there is a fine view of the
lake and of the grey summit of Brebag, the
dividing mountain between Sutherland and
Ross-shire ; and from the solitary shores of

Loch Veattie there is, perhaps, the best view
of Suilvean in Sutherlandshire ; as well as
many spots from which the peaks and precipices of Coulmore and their romantic surroundings present themselves under the most
favourable aspects for the artist.

Loch Borrolan, which is within a stonethrow
of the inn door, is a little more than a mile
long and a third of a mile wide.   It is a comparatively shallow loch, and in many places
reedy and full of weeds.   It is well stocked
with beautiful trout, and also contains a number of char.   One day, I killed, in three hours,
fishing with the fly, forty trout and three
char, weighing eleven pounds.   The same
day, a gentleman staying at the inn, who
devoted the whole day to fishing, had one
hundred trout weighing twenty pounds.   The
landlord told us that as many as two hundred
have been taken by one rod in a single day—
surely an unnecessary slaughter, as one hundred should amply satisfy the craving for
sport of even the keenest angler.

If the falls on the Kirkaig and the Black
Falls between Cama Loch and Loch Veattie
were made passable, salmon would be enabled

to ascend into Loch Borrolan as well as into Lochs Fewin, Veattie, and Cama Loch, as there is no obstruction on the river that flows from Loch Borrolan into Cama Loch. There is a considerable extent of good spawning ground on this river, and likewise on the lower part of the river that issues from Loch Urigill. On the upper part of the latter river there are three falls of considerable height in the space of little more than half-a-mile, which would effectually arrest the upward progress of salmon, but which it would never be worth while to blast merely for the sake of admitting salmon into Loch Urigill.

Loch Urigill is about two miles from Altnakealgach Inn. You follow the high road to the head of Loch Borrolan, and then strike across the moor. There are plenty of small trout on this loch, and the innkeeper has a boat on it. Cama Loch is an excellent fishing loch, and its surroundings are wild and picturesque. It covers an area of about seven hundred acres, and is divided into two irregularly-shaped sheets of water by a rocky peninsula. The upper half is comparatively shallow, and contains a number of wooded

islands, round which the trouting is very
good; the lower half, which stretches away
in the direction of Suilvean, has steeper and
more rocky shores, and is much deeper and
more suitable for trolling than the upper half.
It also contains larger trout. The ordinary
trout on this loch run from three to the pound,
up to two pound each. A short stream connects Cama Loch with the head of Loch
Veattie. Its upper part consists of two fine
streams and pools, which would be favourite
haunts for salmon if they could once be
enabled to ascend so far; then come the
Black Falls, at least fifteen feet high, then a
long, deep, dark pool, and then Loch Veattie.
Loch Veattie is a narrow Loch, about five
miles in length, very remote, and but little
fished, though good baskets may be made
with the fly, and fish of ten pounds weight have
been taken by trolling in it and in a small loch
at the foot of Coulmore, which communicates
with the larger loch on the south side. It is
a five miles' drive from Altnakealgach Inn to
Loch Veattie, and a five miles' row from the
place where you enter the boat to the lower
end of the loch, near which is the best trout-

ing. It is, therefore, advisable to make an early start, and to have two gillies. Loch Veattie is a capital loch for trolling; deep and free from weeds. The banks are in general rocky, and in many places there are large boulders lying under water not far from the shore—just the sort of beach for salmon. More's the pity they cannot reach it. There is a shallow reedy bay, near the foot of the loch, which is one of the best spots for fly-fishing. In and about it the fish are both numerous and large, and, in a westerly or south-westerly breeze, will rise freely. From Altnakealgach the tourist may return south by the Highland Railway, joining it either at Invershin or at Garve. The drive to Garve by Ullapool, though longer, is much more beautiful and varied than that down the valley of the Oykell to Invershin.

An angling and sketching ramble through Sutherland, such as we have endeavoured to describe in the foregoing pages, may easily be made in from six to seven weeks, and the cost need not exceed £1 per day.

TURNBULL AND SPEARS, PRINTERS.

CPSIA information can be obtained at www.ICGtesting.com
Printed in the USA
BVOW04s0645210515

401292BV00022B/129/P